Love Coupons
for Kids

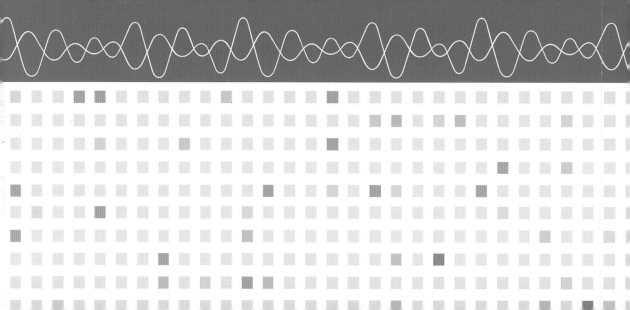

Love Coupons for Kids

52 creative ways to tell your kids how special they are!

by Robin St. John

Andrews McMeel Publishing, LLC

Kansas City

First published in 2002 as *To Kids with Love Coupons* by Hallmark Books, a division of Hallmark Cards, Inc.

09 10 11 LEO 10 9 8 7 6 5 4 3 2

ISBN-13: 978-0-7407-6566-7
ISBN-10: 0-7407-6566-3

www.andrewsmcmeel.com

ATTENTION: SCHOOLS AND BUSINESSES

Andrews McMeel books are available at quantity discounts with bulk purchase for educational, business, or sales promotional use. For information, please write to: Special Sales Department, Andrews McMeel Publishing, LLC, 1130 Walnut St. Kansas City MO 64106.

This coupon is good for one

SUPER-
DUPER
HUG

(Ready whenever you need it!)

This coupon is good for one

EXTRA TREAT

(You can have one more of whatever you were told you've had enough of.)

This coupon is good for staying up

An Hour
Past Your Bedtime

(Read, watch TV, or
whatever you want!)

This coupon is good for

One "Chore-Free"
Saturday

This coupon is good for one

CHOICE
AT THE GROCERY
STORE

(Pick an item and
toss it in the cart!)

This coupon is good for

CONTROL
OF THE TV

(You rule the remote
for a day!)

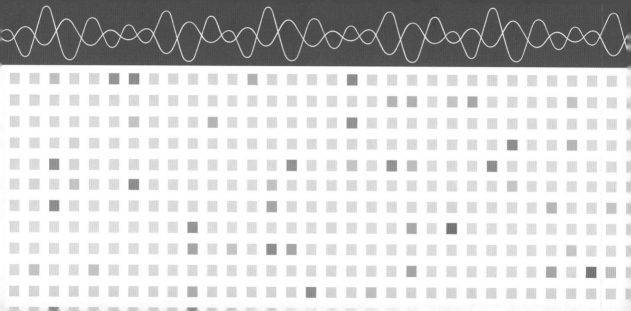

Present this coupon for

A Free CD

by your favorite artist or group

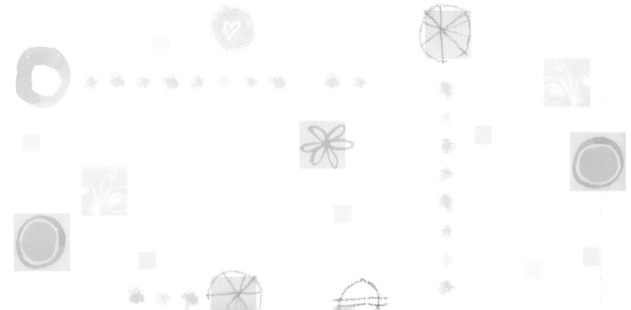

This coupon is good for one

GAME OF YOUR CHOICE

(Pick your favorite board game, sport, or activity!)

This coupon is good for one

MEAL WITH☙UT VEGETABLES

(Say "No Thanks!" to broccoli, Brussels sprouts— even spinach!)

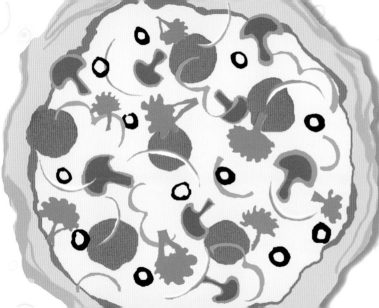

This coupon entitles you to

Choose the **Toppings** on Our **Next Pizza**

(Offer does not apply to Gummy Worms!)

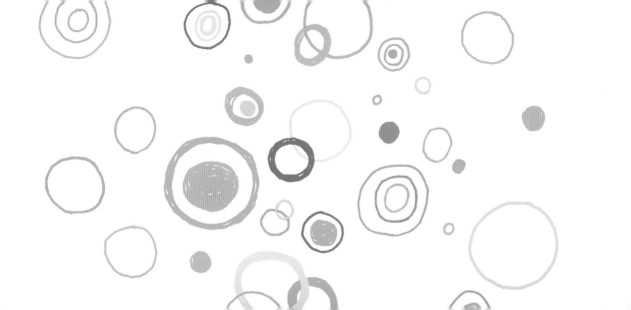

Use this coupon for

One Really Good Story

(Either to be read
or told to you with
all the sound effects!)

This coupon gives you

THE RUN OF THE

VIDEO STORE

Pick your favorite
and the snacks to go with it!

A trip to the
bookstore
or library—or
both!

Use this coupon for

Making your own:

- ice-cream sundae
- sandwich
- decorated cookie

(choose one)

Have fun using all your favorite stuff in the kitchen!

With this coupon you can
select the menu for

A DINNER IN YOUR HONOR!

Use this coupon for

A BACKYARD CAMPOUT

(preferably on a warm night)

This coupon is good for a

NEW BOOK
or GAME

Cash in this coupon for
A TRIP TO THE MALL!

This coupon is good for

An Extra Hour
of Television

This coupon is good for
an afternoon in the outdoors

Hiking, Fishing, Exploring
...whatever
you like!

Trade this coupon in for

A Trip to a
Museum
of Your
Choice

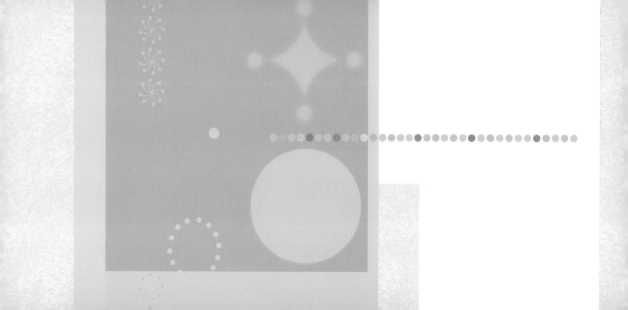

This coupon means

You Don't Have to Clean Your Room for a week!

This coupon entitles you to
A Backyard Cookout

(and you can be the chef,
if you want to!)

This coupon entitles you to

Create an Adventure

(The park, the zoo, the backyard... you choose!)

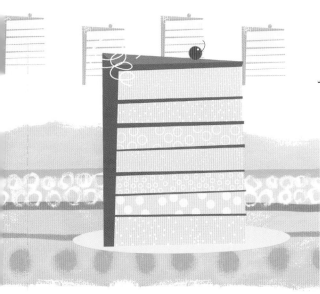

Use this coupon for

The menu of your choice for:

(a) Breakfast
(b) Lunch
(c) Dinner

(choose one)

You get to decide
what we eat for one meal!

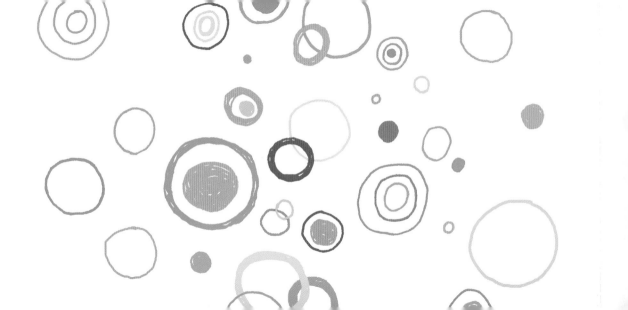

Use this coupon for

(a) A great big hug
(b) A tickling
(c) A hug and a
tickling

(choose one)

(Good for repeats the whole day!)

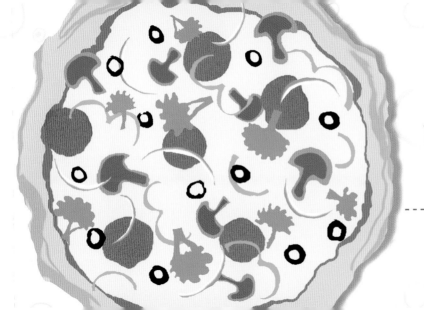

Good
for **one**

- - - - - - - - - - - - - - - - - - -

made to order!

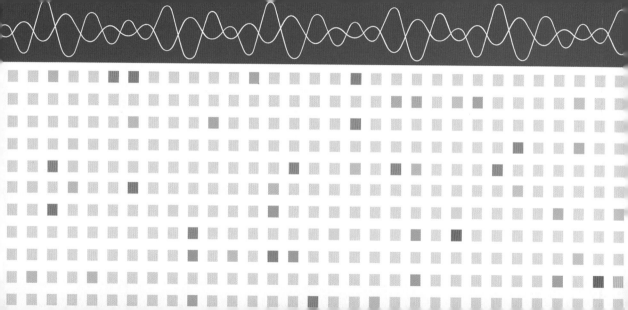

This coupon is good for

FREE TICKETS

for you and a friend

to a concert, movie, or
theme park ... your choice!

This coupon is good for one free

SUNNY FUN DAY!

On the first sunny spring day, get ready to
visit the park or the zoo or have a picnic!

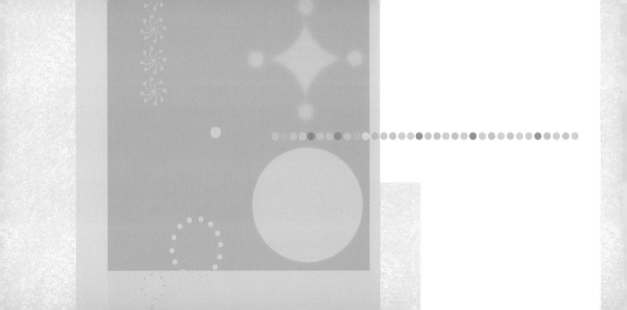

Redeem this coupon for

A NEW POSTER FOR YOUR ROOM

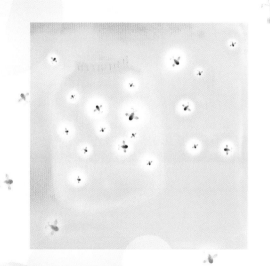

Good for
A SLEEPOVER $z^z{}^z$

with _____ of your
favorite friends.

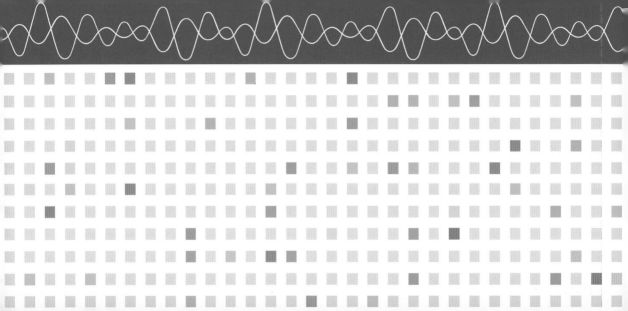

With this coupon you can

Pick the station
on the Car Radio

(Good for one in-town trip!)

This entitles you to

A Fun Class
OR Activity

(Take karate lessons, learn to play a musical instrument, sign up for a sports team ... it's your choice!

This coupon is good for

A BATCH
OF
CKIES

Share or keep all for yourself!

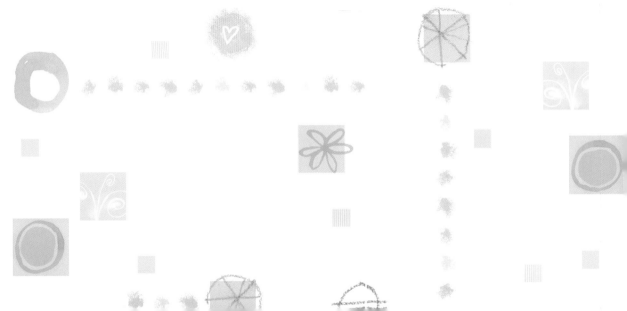

This coupon is worth

A FAMILY GAME NIGHT

(And you get to pick the games!)

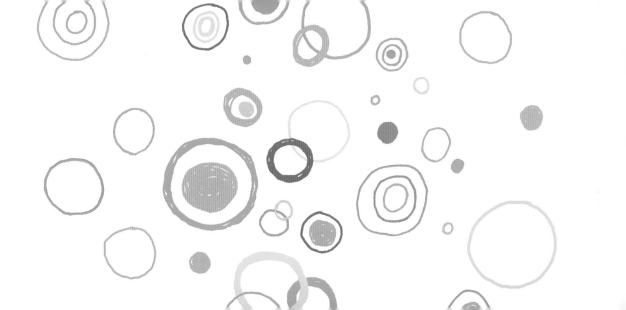

Exchange this coupon for

A SPECIAL
SECRET

(Just between us!)

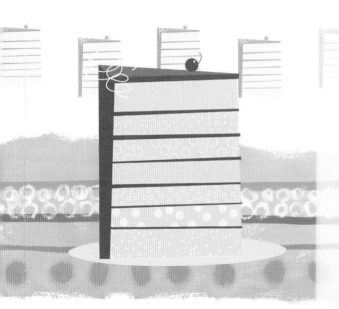

This coupon entitles you to

A CAKE WITH
CANDLES

And you don't have
to wait for your birthday!

(One free wish included!)

This entitles you to

A Day at the Office with Mom or Dad

(Lunch at a cool place included!)

This coupon is good for a

A New Accessory or

 stickers for your "Wheels"

(bike, skateboard, scooter, whatever!)

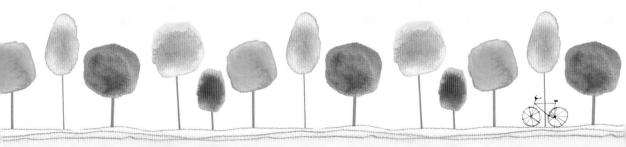

This coupon is good for

CHOCOLATE CHIPS

to be sprinkled on anything you want!

This coupon is good for
One "Chore-Free"
Saturday

This coupon means you can
CHOOSE WHAT
WE DO TODAY

This coupon is good for one

DINNER

OF YOUR CHOICE

(Pick regular or fast food!)

With this coupon you can

PICK
YOUR
WARDROBE
for a week!

Consider this coupon the first deposit to

YOUR VERY OWN

5¢

SAVINGS ACCOUNT

This is good for one day to

EAT WHEREVER YOU WANT

in front of the TV, in your room, outside, even in the garage!

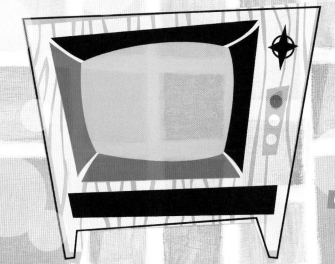

This coupon is good for

One Night of Popcorn and Videos

(You decide what we watch.)

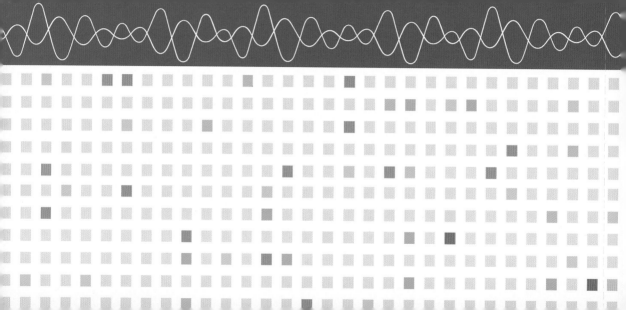

This coupon makes you

a photographer
with your own

DISPOSABLE
CAMERA

Capture your friends,
pets, or family on film.

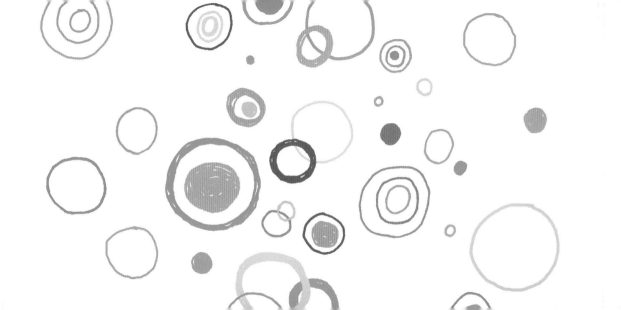

Redeem this for a new

PHOTO ALBUM

to keep the story you created
with your pictures.

Exchange this coupon for

$10 CASH

to spend however you want!

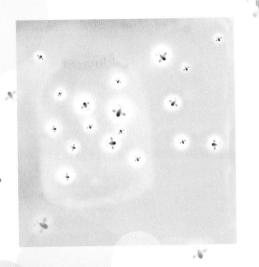

This coupon allows you to

STAY UP
ALL NIGHT

...providing there's no
school the next day.
(Limit one use per customer!)

Special Grown-Up Coupon

This coupon is for the kind adult who purchased this book—this means YOU!

You are hereby entitled to an hour, an afternoon, even a whole day of doing what you enjoy most. After all, you deserve it!